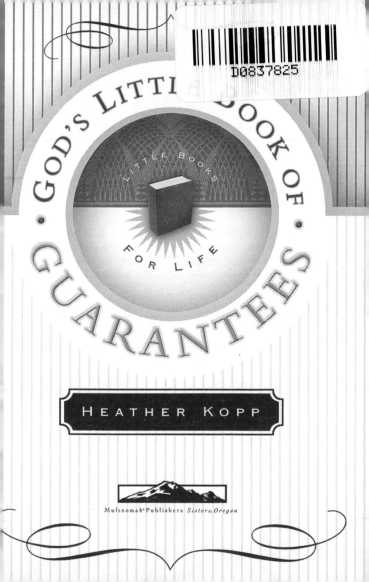

GOD'S LITTLE BOOK OF GUARANTEES

LITTLE BOOKS FOR LIFE

HEATHER KOPP

Multnomah® Publishers *Sisters, Oregon*

GOD'S LITTLE BOOK OF GUARANTEES
published by Multnomah Publishers, Inc.
published in association with the literary agency of
Ann Spangler and Associates
1420 Pontiac Road S.E., Grand Rapids, Michigan 49506

© 2002 by Heather Kopp
ISBN 1-57673-897-3

For information:
MULTNOMAH PUBLISHERS, INC. • P.O. BOX 1720 • SISTERS, OR 97759

Table of Contents

One

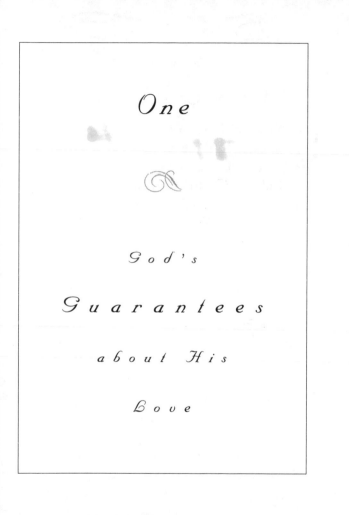

God's

Guarantees

about His

Love

God Guarantees

I HAVE CHOSEN YOU

Always remember that before you ever chose Me, I'd already chosen you to go out into the world and bear fruit for Me that will last forever—making disciples and spreading My Word. If you do this, then you'll be able to ask Me for anything you need in My Son's name, and I will give it to you.

FROM JOHN 15:16

WARRANTY NOTES: IF YOU DO GOD'S WORK, HE PROMISES TO GIVE YOU EVERYTHING YOU NEED TO DO IT.

Dear God,
Thank You for giving me such
an important assignment!
I am anxious to do Your work in the world,
and I trust You to give me everything I
need to accomplish every challenge I face.
Amen.

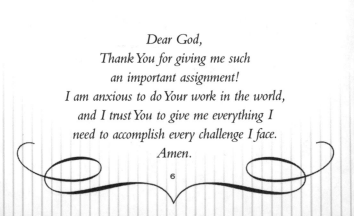

God Guarantees

I LOVED YOU FIRST

If ever you doubt My love, remember what I did to prove it to you. I sent My only Son into the world for you. Think about it: I loved you first—even while you were sinful and didn't love Me. Without your doing anything for Me, I sent My sinless Son to sacrifice His life for your sins. That's why you can always be certain that My love for you doesn't rest on your performance and can't be earned or increased.

FROM 1 JOHN 4:9–10

WARRANTY NOTES: IT'S IMPOSSIBLE FOR GOD TO LOVE YOU MORE THAN HE ALREADY DOES.

Dear God,
How awesome that You love me so completely.
You loved me even before I decided to get to know You.
Keep me safe in Your love today and every day.
Amen.

God Guarantees

I WILL REJOICE
OVER YOU

I, the Lord your God, am with you. I am mighty and able to save you. I want you to be convinced that I take great delight in you. Allow Me, and I will quiet you with My love. I "will rejoice over you with singing."

FROM ZEPHANIAH 3:17

WARRANTY NOTES: THE SONGS OF GOD'S LOVE ARE EVERYWHERE AROUND US, ALL THE TIME.

Dear God,
How amazing it is to know that
You love me so much.
I love to think of You rejoicing over me in song.
Teach me to please You more and more.
Amen.

God Guarantees

YOU ARE MY BELOVED FRIEND

It isn't easy to find a friend—but you can count on Me. I sent My Son for you, and He'll do the things a best friend does. He'll rejoice with you when good things happen; He'll listen when you need to vent; and He'll stick close by when you need help. Follow my commands and call out Jesus' name and He'll be right there.

FROM JOHN 15:12–14

WARRANTY NOTES: FRIENDSHIP WITH GOD NEVER WEARS OUT.

Dear God, thank You for giving me a friend like Jesus. When my earthly friends are not around, Jesus lets me laugh or weep, ramble or rant. Please help me remember that Your Son is near, ready to be my loving friend. Amen.

God Guarantees

I KNOW YOU INTIMATELY

I know everything about you. From far away I know what you're thinking. I'm up-to-date on the details of your life. I'm right beside you—wherever you go. My powerful hands tend to the intricate details of your life. I was there when you were put together. I prepared each day of your life before you were born. I think about you all the time. And I'm ready to lead you to eternal life.

FROM PSALM 139

WARRANTY NOTES: THE ONE WHO KNOWS YOU BEST LOVES YOU MOST.

Dear God, You think about me all the time.
You're always ready and eager to guide me. I can't
comprehend this. When it comes to meeting You, I can't
get it wrong or find myself waiting in the wrong place
or at the wrong time. No matter the place or the time,
You will be there. Show me how to follow You perfectly.
Amen.

God Guarantees

YOU ARE IMPORTANT
TO MY CHURCH

No matter what your gifts or background, you have an important part in the church, My body. Everyone's role is unique, each contribution crucial. Just as with the human body, the head cannot say to the feet, "I don't need you!" Even if you are a part of My body that seems small or inconsequential, you are nevertheless indispensable, and you should treat with special honor and care those members of My body who don't necessarily appear important.

FROM 1 CORINTHIANS 12:18–23

WARRANTY NOTES: TO PREVENT CONTENTION AMONG US, GOD WANTS US TO UNDERSTAND THAT WE ARE ALL EQUALLY IMPORTANT (SEE 1 CORINTHIANS 12:25–26).

Dear God, I am so thankful that You think I am indispensable to Your church. Help me to do my part and to honor the gifts and contributions of others. Amen.

I MAKE NO DISTINCTIONS AMONG YOU

Everyone who puts his or her faith in Christ is a child of God. Because you have been baptized in Christ and clothe yourself with Christ, you are equally My heirs—my sons and daughters. I make no distinction between Jews or Greeks or any other race, or between slaves or free men or any other social status. You all belong to Christ and are heirs of My promises.

FROM GALATIANS 3:28–29

WARRANTY NOTES: THE IDEA OF EQUALITY IN CHRIST WAS REVOLUTIONARY TO THE JEWS WHO FIRST HEARD THESE WORDS (SEE ALSO COLOSSIANS 3:11; 1 CORINTHIANS 12:13).

Dear God, because I am clothed in Christ, I am just as valuable to You as the most famous, rich, or pious Christian. Because in You there is no discrimination, as a result, there should be none among Your children. Amen.

God Guarantees

MY LOVE IS EVERLASTING

The tallest mountains are worn away by time, yet I am the everlasting Rock. My love lasts forever too. You can rely on Me to carry you through any circumstance of life, and I'll never change the way I love you. The steadfastness of My love cannot be eroded or destroyed. Even if you are buffeted by disasters or beaten down by disease, My love will remain. I will care for you with kindness and mercy because I love you with an everlasting love.

FROM ISAIAH 26:4; JEREMIAH 31:3

WARRANTY NOTES: WHEN PEOPLE'S LOVE SEEMS FICKLE AND FADING, REMEMBER THAT GOD'S LOVE IS NOTHING LIKE THAT.

Dear God, every time I think You have forgotten me, I look up and You are there. Please help me remember that life has its ups and downs, but Your love for me is constant and eternal.
Amen.

Two

God's Guarantees about His Provision

God Guarantees

I WILL WITHHOLD NO GOOD THING

I assure you that I will always be your protector and your provider. I'll shine My light in front of you so you'll know which way to go, and I'll shower you with grace so you can stay on the right path. Walk with Me, and I promise I'll never keep good things from your life.

FROM PSALM 84:11

WARRANTY NOTES: IF SOMETHING IS GOOD FOR YOU, GOD WANTS TO GIVE IT TO YOU.

Dear God,
I acknowledge You today, Lord,
as my light and my shield.
Let me walk in the path You set before me.
I want to rely on the good things
You so lovingly supply.
Amen.

God Guarantees

I WILL SUPPLY
ALL YOUR NEEDS

My Son, Jesus, already paid with His life for everything you'll ever need, so I promise to supply what He's purchased for you. Whether you lack basic things like clothes or food, or you're in need of comfort or support, you should ask Me for it in My Son's name, confident that I will be true to My word.

FROM PHILIPPIANS 4:19

WARRANTY NOTES: GOD KNOWS WHAT YOU NEED BETTER THAN YOU DO.

Dear God,
Whether I lack money, food, or other things,
I sometimes forget that You never run out of blessings.
Today I remember that because of Jesus,
You abundantly supply my needs.
Amen.

God Guarantees

I WILL GIVE YOU THE DESIRES OF YOUR HEART

I long to give you the desires of your heart. As you gain greater pleasure in living according to My ways, you'll begin to want the same things I want to give you. Although circumstances may not always happen the way you think they should, you can be confident that I know what your soul cries out for—and I'm happy to provide it.

FROM PSALM 37:4

WARRANTY NOTES: WHEN WE DELIGHT IN THE LORD, OUR HEARTS' DESIRES CHANGE AS A RESULT. THE CLOSER WE COME TO GOD, THE MORE OUR DESIRES REFLECT HIS DESIRES.

Dear God, I believe that You will give me the desires of my heart—my deepest longings, not passing fancies. As I get to know You, teach me to delight in Your ways, and show me the true nature of my hopes and dreams.
Amen.

God Guarantees

I Will Give You All My Benefits

My benefits are better than what any employer could offer, and I promise that if you are Mine, you qualify for all of them. Some of the wonderful things I'll do for you include pardoning your sins and healing your disease. I've redeemed you from hell, and I will shower you with loving-kindness and compassion.

FROM PSALM 103:2–4

WARRANTY NOTES: IF YOU KNOW GOD, YOU ARE ENTITLED TO RECEIVE HIS FULL BENE-FIT PACKAGE, INCLUDING FORGIVENESS, HEALING, REDEMPTION, LOVING-KINDNESS, AND COMPASSION.

Dear God, thank You for being so generous and loving.
I admit that I don't deserve the kinds of gifts You
bestow, but I humbly accept them.
I'm so grateful to know You.
Amen.

God Guarantees

I Will Open the Floodgates of Heaven

If you will give Me your whole tithe, the first 10 percent of all you earn, I promise that I will throw open the floodgates of heaven and pour out so much blessing on you that you won't know what to do with it. Put Me to the test by obeying Me in this, and see what I will do for you!

FROM MALACHI 3:10

Warranty Notes: When you tithe and are blessed in return, others will see what happens and "others will call you blessed" (Malachi 3:12). See also Proverbs 3:9–10.

Dear God, I believe that You will bless me outrageously
if I obediently tithe to You from my income.
I choose to test You in this, confident that in due time
You will bless my faithfulness.
Amen.

God Guarantees

I WILL PROVIDE FOR YOU

Don't worry about what you will eat or drink, or about what you will wear. People who don't know Me spend a lot of time worrying about these things. You know that I'm fully aware of your needs. Instead of fretting about these things, seek My kingdom before anything else and spend your efforts obtaining My righteousness. Then I guarantee you that all these other things will be given to you as well.

FROM MATTHEW 6:31–33

WARRANTY NOTES: REMEMBER WHAT JESUS SAID: "THEREFORE DO NOT WORRY ABOUT TOMORROW, FOR TOMORROW WILL WORRY ABOUT ITSELF" (MATTHEW 6:34).

Dear God, I believe that You are aware of all my needs and will meet them. Teach me to spend my greatest energies pursuing You and Your kingdom. I am fully confident that You will see to my earthly needs as well. Amen.

God Guarantees

YOU WILL LAY UP TREASURES IN HEAVEN

If you are rich in this world, don't put your hope in your wealth—put your hope in Me. I urge you to be rich in good works. If you are generous and willing to share your earthly wealth, I guarantee that you will be laying up a lasting treasure in heaven, which will be a firm foundation for your eternity.

FROM 1 TIMOTHY 6:17–19

WARRANTY NOTES: JESUS URGES YOU TO USE YOUR WORLDLY WEALTH TO MAKE FRIENDS ON EARTH WHO WILL SOMEDAY REMEMBER YOUR GENEROSITY IN HEAVEN (SEE LUKE 16:9).

Dear God, help me approach my finances with the big picture—the eternal picture—in mind. I choose to be generous with my riches and in my actions so that I can claim Your promise of treasure in heaven.

Amen.

Three

God's
Guarantees
about His
Saving Grace

God Guarantees

YOUR SALVATION
RESTS ON GRACE

I promise that it is only by grace you have been saved, through your faith, and not because of anything you did or didn't do. Your forgiveness is a free, unmerited gift from Me, and you can never boast that you earned it. And all those good things you do? They don't happen because of your own goodness either. You are My workmanship, and I created You in Christ Jesus to do good works—works that I prepared in advance for you.

FROM EPHESIANS 2:8–10

WARRANTY NOTES: IF YOU THINK YOU'RE NOT WORTHY OF SALVATION OR DON'T DESERVE IT, YOU'RE RIGHT.

Dear God, I know that if I had to earn my salvation from You, I would never be saved. I agree with You that I am saved by Your amazing, generous, unearned grace. May I always remember this and be thankful.

Amen.

God Guarantees

YOU ARE JUSTIFIED
BY GRACE

Believe Me when I tell you that through My grace you are justified and put in right standing with Me. I promise you freely given favor and mercy, which you haven't earned and can't earn. You are free from guilt because of the redemption that Jesus provided through His death.

FROM ROMANS 3:24

WARRANTY NOTES: WHEN WE ARE JUSTIFIED BY GOD'S GRACE, IT'S "JUST AS IF" WE'D NEVER SINNED.

Dear God, thank You for Your saving grace.
Thank You for providing me redemption from
my sin so that I can stand freely before You,
justified and filled with joy.
Amen.

YOU ARE AN HEIR WITH CHRIST

You are My child. That means you are also My heir and a fellow heir with Christ. Think about it—you share fully in My Son's inheritance. As you grow and become conformed to My will, I invite you to put your hope in your inheritance of eternal life.

FROM TITUS 3:7; ROMANS 8:17

WARRANTY NOTES: HEIRS ARE FULLY ENTITLED TO RECEIVE WHAT IS LEFT TO THEM—PROPERTY AND POSSESSIONS AND WHATEVER ELSE IS OF VALUE. AS AN HEIR, YOU HAVE ONLY TO RECEIVE YOUR INHERITANCE.

Dear God,
I always have the hope of eternal life with You.
I have a share in everything God has given to Christ. I
choose to believe in and receive the full and wonderful
inheritance You have given me.
Amen.

God Guarantees

YOU ARE NOT UNDER LAW, BUT UNDER MY GRACE

Although you constantly struggle with sin, that sin will no longer have any dominion or power over you. This is because you are under My grace now—not under a legal system that used to make you a slave to sin. Through My grace I promise you freedom from the law.

FROM ROMANS 6:14–15

WARRANTY NOTES: GRACE DOESN'T GIVE US FREEDOM TO SIN, BUT FREEDOM FROM SIN.

Dear God,
Thank You for freeing me from the law of sin and death and for taking away the power sin held in my life. I draw on Your grace to keep me from letting sin lure me in and take away the joy of pleasing You.
Amen.

MY GRACE IS SUFFICIENT FOR YOU

My favor and grace are always sufficient to help you when you face trouble of any kind. When you feel most weak, you can be sure that My power is made perfect and complete through your situation. You can even gladly glory in your weakness because My strength and might will rest on you and dwell in you. You will have what you need.

FROM 2 CORINTHIANS 12:9

WARRANTY NOTES: WE CAN REJOICE DURING OUR TIMES OF WEAKNESS, BECAUSE THOSE ARE THE TIMES GOD LOVES TO SHOWS US WHO HE IS.

*Dear God, at times it seems that You let me go through
things I can't imagine making it through.
Just when I think I can't make it, You pick me up
and give me a strength I can only attribute to You.
Thank You for being strong when I am weak.
Amen.*

God Guarantees

You Will Never Be Put to Shame

If you believe in Me and rely on Me, you will never be filled with shame. I have placed beneath you a foundation that is tested and won't move; you will not be ashamed or disappointed.

FROM ROMANS 10:11; ISAIAH 28:16

WARRANTY NOTES: WHEN WE SIN, WE SHOULD FEEL CONVICTED AND BE REPENTANT. BUT BECAUSE OF WHAT JESUS DID, WE DON'T HAVE TO FEEL THAT TERRIBLE SENSE OF SHAME.

Dear God, I can't think of a feeling worse than shame.
How grateful I am for Your promise that I will
not be put to shame because Jesus already took
all my shame upon Himself.
Amen.

God Guarantees

YOU WILL BE SAVED

My salvation is so very near you. It is as close as your own mouth and heart. I assure you, if you acknowledge Jesus is Lord with your lips and believe in your heart what I say, you will be saved. You will pass out of death into new life. You will possess eternal life.

FROM ROMANS 10:8–9; JOHN 5:24

WARRANTY NOTES: JESUS MADE IT AS EASY AS POSSIBLE FOR US TO RECEIVE HIS SALVATION. ONLY TWO STEPS ARE REQUIRED— CONFESS AND BELIEVE.

Lord,
I say to You right now,
I am a sinner who needs You.
I believe that You sent Your Son for my salvation.
Thank You, God, for saving me.
Amen.

God Guarantees

YOU WILL HAVE
EVERLASTING LIFE

I so greatly love the world that I chose to give My
Son—My one and only Son—to you. I promise
that *everyone* who clings to Him will not perish.
You won't be lost, but you will have never-ending
life. I didn't send My Son to condemn or reject
you. I sent Him so you would find My salvation
and life everlasting.

FROM JOHN 3.16–17

**WARRANTY NOTES: THIS PROMISE IS FOR
EVERYONE WHO BELIEVES. ARE YOU PART
OF THE EVERYONE?**

God,
You actually sent Your Son for me, for my salvation.
I am so grateful. You didn't send Him to hurt me or to
pass judgment on me. You had only my best in mind—
saving me from eternal death. Thank You, Lord.
Amen.

God Guarantees

I WILL GIVE YOU MY GLORY

The same glory I gave to My son, Jesus, is now also yours. The same honor and unity I have with Jesus I have with you too. You are joined to all others who believe in Me because of the glory I have given you through My Son. Receive and triumph in the glory that joins us all together.

FROM JOHN 17:22

WARRANTY NOTES: JESUS PLACED SUCH A HIGH VALUE ON THAT HONOR AND GLORY THAT HE CONFIRMED IN PRAYER TO HIS FATHER THAT HE WAS GIVING IT TO US AS A PRECIOUS GIFT.

Dear God, thank You for all the fellow believers You have brought into my life. Sometimes it's easy to take them for granted and not acknowledge their tremendous value. Thank You for Your divine glory, which unifies us all in You.
Amen.

Four

God's

Guarantees

about His

Comfort and

Healing

I WILL COMFORT YOU IN ALL YOUR TROUBLES

I am the Father of mercies and the God of all comfort. Because of these credentials, I can and will comfort you in every trouble you go through. Even in the midst of your greatest struggles, you can find peace and encouragement by letting Me console you. In turn, you will find joy in giving the same comfort to others you encounter who experience similar problems.

FROM 2 CORINTHIANS 1:3–4

WARRANTY NOTES: COMFORT IS NOT THE ANSWER TO A PROBLEM. COMFORT IS THE LOVE AND STRENGTH THAT CARRIES YOU UNTIL AN ANSWER IS FOUND.

Dear God, thank You for those incredible times during my darkest hours when You've wrapped Your arms around me. I believe that You want to comfort me greatly.
Amen.

God Guarantees

I WILL HEAL YOU

When you are in trouble of any kind, you should pray. When you're happy, the right response is to praise Me. When you're sick, you should ask a leader in your church that you respect to pray for you and anoint you with oil in My name. For the prayer that is offered in faith will make you well. I will raise you up from your sickbed, and I will also forgive you of your sins.

FROM JAMES 5:13-15

WARRANTY NOTES: NOT EVERY PRAYER FOR HEALING RESULTS IN COMPLETE AND IMMEDIATE RECOVERY. BUT SINCE GOD TELLS US TO PRAY IN FAITH, WE SHOULD CONTINUE TO DO SO, NO MATTER WHAT THE SYMPTOMS OR CIRCUMSTANCES MAY BE.

*Dear God, You promise to answer the prayer of faith
for healing, so right now I want to boldly ask You
for just that. Thank You for Your promises.
I believe them all, Lord!
Amen.*

God Guarantees

I WILL REVIVE YOU

Though I live in a high and lofty place, this is My promise to you: I also dwell with those who are feeling low in their spirits and who maintain contrite, repentant hearts. When you are feeling depressed and sad, crushed by the weight of life and of your sins, I will revive your spirit and heart.

FROM ISAIAH 57:15

WARRANTY NOTES: KING DAVID WAS STUNNED BY THE FACT THAT GOD ACTUALLY PAYS ATTENTION TO US, MUCH LESS CARES FOR US. HE SAID, "WHAT IS MAN THAT YOU ARE MINDFUL OF HIM, THE SON OF MAN THAT YOU CARE FOR HIM?" (PSALM 8:4).

Dear God,
I long to have a contrite, repentant heart.
Every day, teach me how to respond to my sin in such
a way. Thank You for Your beautiful promise to stay
near to me and to revive my heart with Your love.
Amen.

God Guarantees

MY WORD GIVES LIFE AND HEALTH

My dear child, listen closely to My words. Pay close attention to everything I tell you. I promise you that My words will bring spiritual life to you and vibrant health to your whole body.

FROM PROVERBS 4:20, 22

WARRANTY NOTES: GOD DRAWS A CLEAR CONNECTION BETWEEN OUR SPIRITUAL HEALTH AND OUR PHYSICAL HEALTH.

Dear God,
I confess that I sometimes pay more attention to the latest health fads than I do to Your Word.
Forgive me, please. Thank You that attention to the principles laid out in Your Word will bring me spiritual, and often physical, health.
Amen.

God Guarantees

I WILL NEVER WASTE YOUR TEARS

I have seen you when you're upset and can't sleep. I have collected your tears and put them in a bottle. I have recorded each one in My book. When you cry out to Me, I'll take care of your problems. You can know this because I am for you.

FROM PSALM 56:8–9

WARRANTY NOTES: SOMETIMES WE FEEL LIKE OUR SUFFERING SERVES NO PURPOSE. BUT GOD MAKES IT CLEAR THAT HE WILL NOT LET EVEN ONE TEARDROP BE LOST. HE GATHERS THEM AND USES THEM IN OUR LIVES AND IN THE LIVES OF THOSE AROUND US.

Dear God, I don't like to cry or feel hurt, but I take great comfort in knowing that You will not waste one of my teardrops or one stab of pain in my heart. You will use each one for Your good purposes. Amen.

God Guarantees

BY MY WOUNDS
YOU ARE HEALED

You can be sure that when I [Jesus] died for you, I took on all your infirmities and all your sorrows. I was considered stricken and afflicted by God. But it was all for your sake. It was for your transgressions that I was pierced; it was for your peace that I was punished; and it was for your healing that I was wounded.

FROM ISAIAH 53:4–5

WARRANTY NOTES: JESUS TOOK OUR SINS UPON HIMSELF WHEN HE DIED. HE ALSO TOOK ON ALL OUR INFIRMITIES AND SICKNESSES SO THAT THROUGH HIM WE COULD BE HEALED.

Dear God, I believe that You have the power to heal me. I ask that the healing power that was made available to me when You suffered and died on the cross would be at work in my body this day.
Amen.

God Guarantees

YOU ARE
BEING RENEWED

When you feel discouraged, don't lose heart. Remember that even though outwardly you may be wasting away day by day, on the inside you are being renewed by My power. Your light, temporary troubles are guaranteeing you an eternal glory that far outweighs them all.

FROM 2 CORINTHIANS 4:16–17

WARRANTY NOTES: SECOND CORINTHIANS 4:18 REMINDS US THAT WE ARE TO FIX OUR EYES ON UNSEEN, SPIRITUAL TRUTHS. WHAT IS SEEN IS ONLY TEMPORARY, BUT WHAT IS UNSEEN IS ETERNAL.

Dear God, thank You for refreshing me when I
do not have the strength or desire to go on.
I know that these heartaches and troubles I face
now will seem trivial in the light of eternity and in
the light of the glory I will someday experience.
Amen.

God Guarantees

I WILL HEAL YOUR LAND

If you and all those who are called by My name will humble yourselves and pray and seek My face with all your heart, turning aside from your sins and wicked ways, then I will hear you in heaven. Then you can be certain that I will forgive all your sins and heal your land.

FROM 2 CHRONICLES 7:14

WARRANTY NOTES: GOD RESPONDS TO US ON AN INDIVIDUAL BASIS, BUT HE ALSO RESPONDS TO OUR FAMILIES, OUR COMMUNITIES, OUR CHURCHES, AND EVEN OUR WHOLE NATION.

Dear God, I believe that You want to heal not just me, but my entire country. Please move in all of our hearts and minds to turn us to repentance so that You can heal our land of its wounds and diseases, both physical and spiritual.
Amen.

I WILL BE NEAR TO YOU

My eyes are always resting on My righteous people, and when they cry out to Me, I hear them and deliver them. I promise that I will stay especially close to you who are brokenhearted, and I will save any of My children who are crushed in spirit.

FROM PSALM 34:15, 17–18

WARRANTY NOTES: GOD HAS A SOFT HEART FOR HIS CHILDREN WHO ARE IN A ROUGH SPOT.

Dear God,
Because I believe Your promise,
I cry out to You right now and ask You
to draw close to me.
When I feel crushed in spirit,
I pray that You will save me from despair.
Amen.

Five

&

God's Guarantees about His Response to Prayer

God Guarantees

YOUR FAITH CAN MOVE MOUNTAINS

Believe Me when I tell you that if you say to a mountain, "Go, throw yourself into the sea," and do not have doubt in your heart but are convinced that what you've said will happen, it will be done. I tell you, whatever you ask for in prayer, believe that you have already received it, and I promise that it will be yours.

FROM MARK 11:23–24

WARRANTY NOTES: MARK 11:25 GOES ON TO REMIND US THAT WHEN WE ARE PRAYING, WE SHOULD GIVE UP ANY GRUDGES WE'RE HOLDING. IF WE FORGIVE OTHERS, GOD WILL FORGIVE US.

Dear God,
I know that my faith is small, but You are great.
Give me greater faith—and help me not to doubt.
And I believe in my heart that I have already received it.
Amen.

I WILL ACCEPT YOUR PRAYER

When you feel unworthy, come to Me. I will accept your prayer and hear your cry for mercy. Rest assured that I will never reject your prayer for help, and I will never withhold My love from you.

FROM PSALM 6:9; 66:20

WARRANTY NOTES: PSALM 66:18 REMINDS US NOT TO CHERISH ANY SIN IN OUR HEARTS SO THAT NOTHING WILL PREVENT GOD FROM LISTENING TO OUR PRAYERS.

Dear God,
I believe that You accept my prayer and that when
I cry out for mercy, You come rushing to my side.
How wonderful it is to know that unlike fickle
humans, You will never reject me or be stingy
with Your love. Thank You, Lord.
Amen.

God Guarantees

I Know What You Need

When you pray, don't make a public show of it, but pray to Me in private. I'm not interested in rote or lengthy prayers, but in genuine prayers from your heart. The reason I want you to pray to Me is not because I don't know what you need. I already know very well what your needs are. I ask you to pray because I long to converse with you as part of a personal and intimate relationship.

FROM MATTHEW 6:6–8

WARRANTY NOTES: PRAYER IS NOT A PERFORMANCE, BUT A PRIVATE CONVERSATION.

Dear God, thank You that You already know what I need, and yet You invite me to tell You about it just the same. In response, may my prayers always be heartfelt and honest, not mechanical or shallow. I pray that our talks will continually bring us closer together.
Amen.

God Guarantees

YOU WILL FIND ME

I never hide from you, nor am I reluctant to answer you. Only ask of Me and it will be given to you. Seek Me and you will find Me. Knock on My door and I will gladly open it to you. For everyone who asks receives. Everyone who seeks finds. And for everyone who knocks on My door, I will throw it wide open.

FROM MATTHEW 7:7–8

WARRANTY NOTES: GOD IS ALWAYS PURSUING US, AND HE WANTS US LIKEWISE TO PURSUE HIM.

Dear God,
If I will only seek You,
You promise that I will find You.
What wonderful news!
Today I will seek You out and knock on Your door,
knowing that You will not fail to open it to me.
Amen.

God Guarantees

I WILL GIVE YOU GOOD GIFTS

When you doubt My generous nature, think about this: If your child asked for bread, would you give him a stone? Or if he asked for a fish, would you give him a snake instead? If you, being human and sinful, know how to give good gifts to your children, you can be certain that I, your heavenly Father, will give good gifts to you when you ask.

FROM MATTHEW 7:9–11

WARRANTY NOTES: WHENEVER WE FEEL UNCERTAIN ABOUT GOD'S INTENTIONS IN ANY AREA, IT HELPS TO ASK, "WHAT WOULD A LOVING FATHER DO?"

Dear God, I am so blessed that You already know what I need. You even know what I'm about to think, yet You still invite me to talk to You in prayer. Knowing this, I will make every effort to be sincere and to keep my motives pleasing to You.

Amen.

God Guarantees

I WILL BE PRESENT WITH YOU

If you and another person agree together on earth about what you're asking of Me in heaven, I promise I will do it for you. I assure you that whenever two or three people come together in My name, I am present there with them.

FROM MATTHEW 18:19–20

WARRANTY NOTES: JESUS' PRESENCE AND POWER ARE MANIFEST IN A SPECIAL WAY WHEN TWO OR MORE PEOPLE COME TOGETHER IN HIS NAME.

Dear God,
How wonderful it is to know that when I join with
another person in prayer and we desire the same thing
of You, You will be present with us and answer us.
I believe this with all my heart, and I intend to take
advantage of Your promise soon.
Amen.

God Guarantees

I Am Able to Do More than You Can Ask or Imagine

I have abundant resources. I am the source of all-surpassing strength. I dwell in your heart through faith. When you ask Me for something, ask big. For I am able and willing to do far more than you can ask or imagine.

FROM EPHESIANS 3:20

WARRANTY NOTES: WITH GOD, IT'S IMPOSSIBLE TO EXPECT TOO MUCH, ONLY TOO LITTLE.

Dear God, You are great and powerful.
All the resources in heaven and earth are Yours.
I will stop praying as if I were pleading with someone
who is stingy and unwilling to help, for You are a
gracious and generous Father. Thank You that You are
able to do more for me than I can even imagine.
Amen.

Six

God's
Guarantees
about His
Guidance

God Guarantees

MY HOLY SPIRIT WILL COUNSEL YOU

Even though I am not with you in body, I will send My Holy Spirit to you. He will be a counselor to you, teaching you spiritual truths that you need to know. He will remind you of what I have said in My Word, and He will guide you in the way you should go.

FROM JOHN 14:25–26

WARRANTY NOTES: WHEN WAS THE LAST TIME YOU CONSULTED THE BEST COUNSELOR IN THE WORLD (SEE JOHN 16:13–14)?

Dear God,
I believe that You have indeed sent the Holy Spirit to
live within me and to speak truth to my heart.
Thank You so much. I will ask Him for guidance, confident
that He will help me like no other person could.
Amen.

God Guarantees

I Will Lead You
in the Right Way

When you find yourself facing a dilemma, wait for My instruction. I promise that I will let you know which way you should go. I am a watchful, protective Teacher. I'm always on time with wise counsel. Listen for My directions.

From Psalm 32:8–9

Warranty Notes: No one likes to have to ask for directions, but God wants us to ask before we even begin the trip.

Dear God,
Sometimes I'd rather do my own thing and
go my own way than look to You for instruction.
Forgive my stubbornness. Clear my desires out of the
way when they are roadblocks to Your purposes.
Help me eagerly respond to Your directions.
Amen.

God Guarantees

I WILL GIVE YOU DIRECTIONS

I long to be your gracious guide. I'm waiting for you to ask for directions. As soon as I hear you ask, I'll direct you. No matter which way you go—whether you turn right or left—you will hear My voice. I'll be right beside you, showing you the way to go and encouraging you on your journey.

FROM ISAIAH 30:21

WARRANTY NOTES: IT'S IMPOSSIBLE TO GET LOST IF WE'RE FOLLOWING GOD'S DIRECTIONS.

Dear God, in love, You wait for me to turn to You.
You are so respectful; You won't force Your
ways or commands on me. You wait for me to
solicit Your expertise. Help me turn to You quickly.
When I hear Your voice, don't let me doubt that it's You.
Place Your hand on me and show me Your perfect path.
Amen.

God Guarantees

I WILL GO WITH YOU

Don't let people or circumstances dissuade you from completing the tasks I've assigned you. I'll be right beside you as you face the challenges. Don't be afraid. Be courageous. Act from a position of strength; know that wherever you go, whatever you face, I will go with you. I'll never forget you. I'll continually think of ways to help you.

FROM DEUTERONOMY 31:6

WARRANTY NOTES: JUST AS GOD ENCOURAGED THE ISRAELITES TO GO BOLDLY INTO THE PROMISED LAND, HE ENCOURAGES YOU TO DO WHATEVER HE TELLS YOU WITHOUT BEING AFRAID.

Dear God, I fear that I'm not up to meeting the challenges that lie ahead of me. I find comfort in Your promise to be right beside me, to be my strength as I endeavor to complete the work You've given me. Thank You for Your supernatural strength and help. Amen.

God Guarantees

I Will Give You Wisdom

If you don't know how to handle a situation, just ask Me for wisdom, and I promise that I will give it to you. You can be sure that I generously give wisdom to every person who asks Me for it, and I never fault them for needing My guidance.

FROM JAMES 1:5

WARRANTY NOTES: GOD SAYS THAT WHEN YOU ASK HIM FOR WISDOM, YOU MUST BELIEVE AND NOT DOUBT THAT HE WILL GIVE IT TO YOU (SEE JAMES 1:6).

Dear God,
You've given Your word that if I simply
ask for wisdom, You will give it to me.
I thank You for that promise.
I especially need wisdom concerning _____.
Right now I am asking in faith for You to give me the
discernment I need to make godly decisions.
Amen.

God Guarantees

I WILL LEAD YOU WHEN THE WAY IS UNFAMILIAR

When you face unfamiliar circumstances and can't figure out what to do, when you feel blind, I will lead you. I will turn the darkness into light for you. When the way gets rough, I will go in front and smooth it so you do not stumble.

FROM ISAIAH 42:16

WARRANTY NOTES: WHEN YOU FEEL BLIND AND IN THE DARK, REMEMBER THAT GOD SEES EVERYTHING IN ITS FULLEST LIGHT.

Dear God,
I am so bewildered.
I don't know what to do concerning _____.
But I know that You have designed my life according to
Your great plans. I believe that the less I'm able
to see, the tighter You hold my hand.
Amen.

God Guarantees

WHAT I PLAN
WILL TAKE PLACE

When you are uncertain, remember that if I intend to do something in your life, it will happen. You can rest assured that whatever I have said to you, I will bring about. I promise that what I have planned for you will take place.

FROM ISAIAH 46:11

WARRANTY NOTES: IF GOD HAS A PLAN, IT'S IMPOSSIBLE FOR YOU TO GET IN HIS WAY.

Dear God,
I thank You that if You are up to
something in my life,
even if I don't quite understand,
even if I make a wrong move,
You are bigger than that.
What You decide is what will happen.
Amen.

God Guarantees

I WILL DIRECT
YOUR PATHS

If you trust Me unreservedly, I will clearly show you where to go. Don't try to figure it out by yourself. I promise that even when My ways don't make sense to you, I am guiding you along the best of all possible paths.

FROM PROVERBS 3:5-6

WARRANTY NOTES: GOD NOT ONLY GIVES US DIRECTION, BUT ALSO ACTUALLY GOES BEFORE US, PREPARING THE PATH FOR US.

Dear God,
It is so reassuring to envision You going ahead of me,
shaping the turns in the road,
dealing with obstacles that would block my path.
I believe that You are in charge of
my entire life's journey.
Amen.

Seven

❦

God's
Guarantees
about His
Word

God Guarantees

YOU WILL FIND
GREAT REWARD

All My commandments and principles, which you can find in My Word, are absolutely solid and perfectly righteous. They are more precious than gold, than much pure gold; they are sweeter than honey is to your mouth. When you know My words, you will be warned to stay away from evil; and when you obey them, I promise that you will find great reward.

FROM PSALM 19:9–11

WARRANTY NOTES: IT IS GOOD TO HAVE A SWEET TOOTH FOR GOD'S WORD.

Dear God,
Thank You for Your statutes. Give me a spiritual hunger
and satisfy it with Your sweet Word. Teach me all I need
to know to avoid evil. I will follow Your commands and
look for Your reward.
Amen.

God Guarantees

My Word Will Last Forever

My Word is eternal. You can rely on My promises forever. They will never let you down. You can count on Me to keep My Word, even when the sky and earth disappear.

FROM MARK 13:31

WARRANTY NOTES: GOD'S ETERNALLY RELIABLE WORD IS MORE AVAILABLE AND ACCESSIBLE TODAY THAN AT ANY OTHER TIME IN THE WORLD'S HISTORY.

*Dear God,
I feel so let down when a friend
breaks an important promise.
Thank You that I can count on
You to always keep Your Word.
I can rely on every promise You've ever uttered.
Amen.*

MY WORD IS GOOD
FOR INSTRUCTION

I have breathed life into all My words. That is why you can know for certain that they will teach you what is true. Rely on Scripture to reveal what is wrong in your life and to help you set things straight. When you pay attention to My words, you can be certain that you will learn to please Me. My instruction will prepare you for life and equip you for every good work.

FROM 2 TIMOTHY 3:16–17

WARRANTY NOTES: EVEN THOUGH MANY DIFFERENT WRITERS ACTUALLY PUT THE WORDS ON PAPER TO CREATE THE BIBLE, WE CAN REST ASSURED THAT GOD INSPIRED THEM.

Dear God, I believe that all of the words in Your Bible are Your words. Through Your Word and by Your Spirit, please help me to want to do right. Make me eager to serve You and to do all the good works You'd like me to do.

Amen.

God Guarantees

MY WORD WILL BE FULFILLED

Not one single letter or word of My Law will be lost or fade away without being fulfilled. You can be confident that every single detail, even the smallest one, will be accomplished until all My purposes have been achieved.

FROM MATTHEW 5:18

WARRANTY NOTES: GOD'S WILL, WHICH HE OUTLINED IN THE BIBLE, WILL BE ACCOMPLISHED IN DUE TIME.

Dear God,
It is good to know that no matter what goes on in this world, no matter how things look, You are in control—
You're not worried that Your plans could fail.
Not in the slightest. I choose to share Your confidence about this today.
Amen.

God Guarantees

MY WORD IS A TWO-EDGED SWORD

My Word is full of living power. It is sharper than the sharpest sword. It will discern your thoughts and intentions. I promise you that if you let My Word into your heart, it will reveal what is really there, whether good or bad.

FROM HEBREWS 4:12

WARRANTY NOTES: UNTIL WE LET GOD PIERCE OUR HEART WITH THE TRUTH, WE CANNOT BEGIN TO HEAL OR CHANGE.

Dear God,
Your Word can penetrate my thoughts
and turn them toward You.
Your Word discerns my intentions and helps me learn to
please You from the very center of my being.
Thank You for the living power of Your Word.
Amen.

God Guarantees

MY WORD WILL LIGHT YOUR PATH

My word is like a lamp that you can use to light your path. When your way seems dark or confused, turn to My instructions. They will shed fresh light on what you should do. When you think on My words, your understanding is sure to be illuminated.

FROM PSALM 119:105, 130

WARRANTY NOTES: IF YOU WANT TO LEARN MORE ABOUT THE POWER OF GOD'S WORD, READ EVERY WORD OF PSALM 119.

Dear God,
When I am stumbling through
the darkness, please light my path.
I know that You keep Your promises.
I will wait for understanding from You,
especially about _____.
Amen.

God Guarantees

MY WORD MAKES YOU PURE

If you want to live a pure life, read My Word and obey it. When you study My ways and live according to them, you will discover that you are living a clean, pure life. My words can clean the inmost parts of your spirit.

FROM PSALM 119:9

WARRANTY NOTES: SINKING INTO GOD'S WORD IS LIKE TAKING A SPIRITUAL BATH.

Dear God,
My mind is so contaminated with the values
of our culture and my own selfish impulses.
Please use the words I read today to clean my mind.
Purify my heart and spirit as You have promised to do.
And I will love You, as You so deserve to be loved.
Amen.

God Guarantees

MY WORD IS
IN YOUR HEART

When you look for Me, you will find Me. When you want to hear My words, you will hear Me speaking. It is not as hard as you imagine to figure out what I am saying. My Word is near you. It is in your mouth and on your heart. I want you to be sure of it so that you can obey it.

FROM DEUTERONOMY 30:14

WARRANTY NOTES: JEREMIAH DECLARED THAT GOD WANTS TO WRITE HIS LAW ON OUR HEARTS (SEE JEREMIAH 31:33).

Dear God,
Your Word is clear.
It's not vague or puzzling.
You've given me clear instructions.
Thank You for making Your ways obvious to me.
Amen.

God Guarantees

MY WORD WILL
NOT RETURN EMPTY

I send the rain and snow to the thirsty earth to water it. The moisture does what I intend. Grain grows, producing seed for the farmer and bread for the hungry. I get similar results when I send out My Word. Be confident that when My Word is sent out, it is powerful, and it will yield results. My Word will always accomplish what I intend.

FROM ISAIAH 55:10–11

WARRANTY NOTES: A WELL-KNOWN PROVERB SAYS, "THE PROMISE OF A GOOD MAN BECOMES AN OBLIGATION." GOD IS SO MUCH GREATER THAN A GOOD MAN.

Dear God, it's reassuring to know that whenever I tuck a piece of Your Word into my heart, something happens. Your words never fall to the ground and die, but always produce something good. Because I know this, I will plant the seed of Your Word wherever I can.

Amen.

Eight

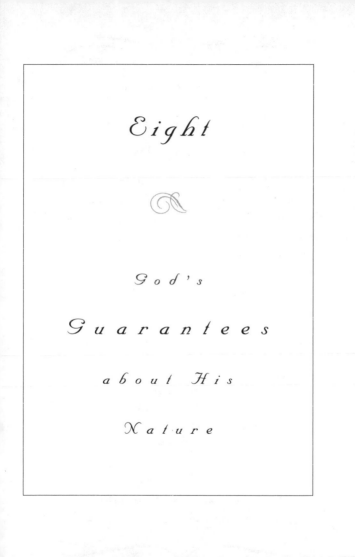

God's

Guarantees

about His

Nature

God Guarantees

I AM THE ALMIGHTY CREATOR

I am the Author of everything—from far-off galaxies to the smallest creature on earth. I created the universe for My own enjoyment, and there is no power above Me. But I promise that I will never be too busy to notice you. Walk with Me and do what I ask, and I assure you that you'll receive My blessings.

FROM GENESIS 17:1; COLOSSIANS 1:16

WARRANTY NOTES: GOD PROMISED ABRAHAM THAT IF HE WOULD OBEY AND DO RIGHT, GOD WOULD ENTER INTO A CONTRACT OF BLESSINGS WITH HIM. WHEN WE DECIDE TO OBEY, GOD BLESSES OUR LIVES TOO.

Dear God,
Wherever I look, I see the amazing universe You made.
The beauty of Your creation surrounds me, and I'm in
awe. May I always serve You, almighty God.
Amen.

God Guarantees

I Am Patient

I promise to be patient with you, as a loving parent is patient with his children. I long for you to know My Son, Jesus. Because a thousand years is like a day to Me, I guarantee that I won't get tired of waiting for you to repent and join My family.

FROM 2 PETER 3:9

WARRANTY NOTES: GOD WAITED FOR NOAH TO FINISH THE ARK BEFORE HE BROUGHT THE FLOOD UPON THE EARTH. GOD IS PATIENT WITH US BECAUSE HE LONGS FOR EVERYONE TO ACCEPT JESUS AND BE SAVED.

Dear God,
Thank You that, unlike me, You are always patient,
always long-suffering. I believe that just as You wait
patiently for Your children to come to salvation,
You continue to be patient with the spiritual
progress of those who already have.
Amen.

God Guarantees

I AM HOLY

You can be certain that I am blameless and perfect—that is, holy. Some have worshiped gods that were capricious, but I am pure and sinless. You can trust Me in every way. I've given My holiness to My Son, Jesus, and He will always lead you away from sin and closer to Me.

FROM ISAIAH 6:3; LEVITICUS 19:2

WARRANTY NOTES: 1 PETER 1:15 REMINDS US THAT BECAUSE GOD IS HOLY, WE TOO SHOULD STRIVE TO BE HOLY.

Dear God,
I believe that because You are holy,
I can always trust You.
Thank You for making me holy in Jesus,
and help me to strive to be holy in all I do.
Amen.

God Guarantees

I Am Just

Life isn't fair, but you can be sure that I am just. I promise that I will never change the rules or falsely accuse you. I've given to My Son, Jesus, the authority to judge, and you can rely on Him to be evenhanded too. Plead your case before Jesus and He will always be honest and trustworthy.

FROM JOHN 5:30

WARRANTY NOTES: GOD IS NOT ONLY JUST, BUT ALSO A LOVER OF JUSTICE WHO WANTS US TO BE JUST (SEE ISAIAH 61:8).

Dear God,
I believe that You are a just God—
and that You sent Jesus to listen to all
my complaints and concerns.
When life isn't fair,
help me remember to trust Your judgment.
Amen.

God Guarantees

I Am Full of Mercy

I promise to have mercy on you because of My great love for you. My rich mercy is what saved you when you were dead in sin, so that you could be made alive in Christ once and for all. I love you so much that each day My mercies for you are brand-new all over again. I will never run out of mercy for you.

FROM EPHESIANS 2:4–5; LAMENTATIONS 3:22–23

WARRANTY NOTES: JESUS TOLD US TO BE MERCIFUL, JUST AS OUR FATHER IS MERCIFUL (SEE LUKE 6:36).

Dear God,
I am so grateful for Your mercy.
Without it, I would never be able to stand before You.
Help me to be merciful to those I meet today.
Amen.

God Guarantees

MY SON IS YOUR COUNSELOR

Another name for My Son, Jesus, is Wonderful Counselor. I promise that if you need someone to talk to, He will listen. He will represent you when you come before My throne, and He will always give you sound advice. I promise that He will counsel you with your best interests in mind. And when you come before Me, just say that you come in the name of Jesus—I promise to hear you.

FROM ISAIAH 9:6

WARRANTY NOTES: OUR COUNSELOR, JESUS, IS ALWAYS READY TO TALK WITH US ABOUT ANY PROBLEM WE HAVE.

Dear God,
Sometimes I feel as if no one understands my problems.
It's wonderful to know that I can tell Jesus about my
innermost troubles and He'll always be available to
point me in the right direction.
Amen.

God Guarantees

I Am Light

You can believe that I am full of light and that there is no darkness in Me at all. I am the One who said, "Let there be light." The sun rises and sets at My command. I even gave you My Word to be a light for your path. I promise that My light will steer you away from the dangers of sin and brighten the high road as you walk with Me. My light is eternal and guaranteed never to fade or become dark.

FROM JOHN 8:12; PSALM 119:105

WARRANTY NOTES: THE BIBLE IS GOD'S FLASHLIGHT, SHINING TRUTH AND WISDOM ON THE PATHWAY OF ALL WHO BELIEVE IN HIS PROMISES.

Dear God, thank You for Your promise to light my way.
Because You are completely full of light
and You live inside Me, I never have to be
afraid of losing my way in the dark.
Amen.

God Guarantees

I AM PEACE

My Son, Jesus, is the Prince of Peace. He makes peace on earth possible. Believe Me when I tell you that Jesus is the only way to peace—for yourself, other people, and the whole world. I promise you that the peace of Jesus is more than just the absence of fighting. It passes all understanding, and it is a gift I offer freely to anyone who accepts Jesus Christ as Lord and Savior.

FROM EPHESIANS 2.14;
ISAIAH 9:6; PHILIPPIANS 4:7

WARRANTY NOTES: IN A WAR-TORN WORLD, THE PEACE OF JESUS IS ABLE TO BRING PEOPLE TOGETHER. WITH HIS PEACE, WE CAN BEGIN TO HEAL OUR DIFFERENCES.

*Dear God, when I am troubled or anxious,
angry or afraid, I can find peace in You because
Your very nature is that of peace. Thank You for such
a wonderful gift. Teach me to seek Your peace,
and may others see it in me.*
Amen.

God Guarantees

I AM YOUR FATHER

You have My Word that I am your everlasting and eternal Father, and I promise to love and care for you until time itself passes away. Because My Son died for you, He opened a way for us to be more intimate than ever—so that you can literally call Me "Daddy" and so that I am able to treat you as My beloved child.

FROM ISAIAH 9:6; ROMANS 8:15; GALATIANS 4:6

WARRANTY NOTES: IF YOU DIDN'T HAVE A LOVING EARTHLY FATHER, ASK GOD TO HELP YOU UNDERSTAND HOW HE IS DIFFERENT AND TO ALLOW YOU TO EXPERIENCE WHAT A LOVING FATHER IS REALLY LIKE.

Dear God,
I am so grateful that You would
invite me to call You my Father. When I need a
"daddy," I will remember that You are available.
I will come to You with my needs.
Amen.

Nine

⌘

God's Guarantees about His Care

God Guarantees

I Am Your Shepherd

I am the Good Shepherd. As one of My precious sheep, you recognize My voice. You know Me and I know you intimately. And because I love you so much, My Son willingly laid down His life to save you, along with all My other sheep. No one forced Him to do this, but He chose to do it because I asked Him to.

FROM JOHN 10:14–18

WARRANTY NOTES: GOD'S ANALOGY OF JESUS AS A SHEPHERD WITH HIS SHEEP IS SIGNIFICANT BECAUSE IT IMPLIES A GREAT LEVEL OF CARE AND ATTENTIVENESS. SHEEP HAVE FEW DEFENSES, SO THOSE WHO TEND THEM MUST GUARD AND PROTECT THEM MORE CLOSELY THAN OTHER ANIMALS.

Dear God, I believe that You are indeed my shepherd and that You lovingly watch out for me and provide for me. I pray that I will recognize Your voice more and more and will never stray away from Your loving care.
Amen.

God Guarantees

I WILL CARRY
YOUR CARES

Take all the problems that are making you anxious and weighing you down, and cast them upon My shoulders. Rest assured that you don't need to bear them any longer. I promise that I am strong enough to carry all your burdens. I long to carry them because I care for you.

FROM 1 PETER 5:7

WARRANTY NOTES: GOD'S OFFER TO CARRY OUR BURDENS AND PROBLEMS CAN BE OF BENEFIT TO US ONLY WHEN WE LET GO OF THEM AND ACTUALLY LET HIM TAKE THEM.

Dear God, Your willingness to help me is not the issue. The problem lies in my willingness to let You. Gently pry each of my fingers away from my cares. Help me release anything and everything that I cannot fix or change. Thank You for taking my burdens and for being a real shoulder I can lean on.
Amen.

God Guarantees

I WILL SATISFY YOUR SPIRIT

When your soul is thirsty and hungry, why do you try to satisfy it with store-bought sustenance? Why waste your money and energy trying to buy what can't be bought at all? Come to Me when you are hungry and thirsty of heart. Listen to My words and eat what is truly good for your soul. Then I promise that your soul will delight in the richest of fare and your spirit will finally be satisfied.

FROM ISAIAH 55:1–2

WARRANTY NOTES: THE WAY TO YOUR HEART IS NOT THROUGH YOUR MOUTH OR POCKETBOOK.

Dear God, why do I try to find spiritual satisfaction in earthly pleasures? Thank You for promising me that if I will make Your words the sustenance of my soul, my deepest hungers will finally be satisfied. Today I come to You, confident that I will feast on Your richest provisions.
Amen.

I WILL MAKE ALL GRACE ABOUND TO YOU

If you desire to serve Me with a generous heart, I am able to make all grace abound to you so that in every situation and at all times you will have everything you need. That way you can flourish in every good work that you do for Me.

FROM 2 CORINTHIANS 9:8

WARRANTY NOTES: WHEN WE GIVE GENER-OUSLY OF OUR RESOURCES AND OURSELVES TO OTHERS, GOD IS MOTIVATED TO MAKE SURE WE HAVE ALL WE NEED, WITH PLENTY LEFT OVER.

Dear God, I desire with all my heart to give generously to Your people and to do good works in Your name. I believe that You are indeed able to make all grace abound to me in every way, so that I can do good works every day.
Amen.

God Guarantees

I WILL RESTORE YOUR SOUL

When your heart feels heavy, overwhelmed, worn-out, I promise to bring refreshment to your soul. I will make you rest where it is quiet and peaceful. I will lead you to where you can be renewed. I will restore your soul to a state of health and soundness.

FROM PSALM 23:2–3

WARRANTY NOTES: THE BUSY PACE OF OUR LIVES FIGHTS AGAINST GOD'S DESIRE TO RESTORE OUR SOULS. BUT WE DON'T NEED TO LIVE IN A MONASTERY TO THINK DEEPLY, LISTEN EARNESTLY, AND SPEAK CANDIDLY WITH GOD. WE JUST NEED TO ASK GOD FOR A "GREEN PASTURE" IN THE MIDST OF EACH DAY.

Dear God, my busyness leaves me so drained and worn down. But You have promised me a place of rest and nourishment. Open my eyes so I can find it.
Amen.

I WILL MAKE YOUR STEPS FIRM

If I delight in the way you are walking with Me, I will make your steps firm. Though you stumble now and then and make mistakes, rest assured that you will rise up, because I am with you. Know that I will never stop offering you My hand to support you in every step you take.

FROM PSALM 37:23–24; PROVERBS 24:16

WARRANTY NOTES: CONTRARY TO HOW WE SOMETIMES FEEL, GODLY SUCCESS IS NOT MEASURED BY A LACK OF MISTAKES. IT IS MEASURED BY HOW READILY WE ASK GOD TO HELP US AFTER WE MAKE THEM.

*Dear God, when I stumble in some way,
it is reassuring to know that You don't abandon me.
Instead, You keep reaching out Your steady
hand to support me and help me.
Thank You!
Amen.*

I WILL FILL YOUR LIFE
WITH ABUNDANCE

There are so many things that can kill, steal, and destroy your joy and fulfillment in life. I have come to earth so that you can live with abundance—not just a life of putting one foot in front of the other, but a life filled with purpose and meaning and overflowing with plenty. You can rest assured that I am a God of generosity and abundance.

FROM JOHN 10:10

WARRANTY NOTES: THE ABUNDANT LIFE GOD PROMISES US IS NOT DEPENDENT UPON OUR CIRCUMSTANCES. IT IS ONLY DEPENDENT UPON OUR LOVE RELATIONSHIP WITH GOD.

Dear God, help me not to just plod along in life, but to experience Your abundance and the joy it brings. Open my heart to Your great love and help me discover the adventure of facing each day's events, emotions, and encounters with You by my side.

Amen.

God Guarantees

I WILL ENCOURAGE
YOUR HEART

Because I love you, I want to give you eternal encouragement and good hope. My encouragement is greater than what any other person could offer. I promise to strengthen and encourage your heart.

FROM 2 THESSALONIANS 2:16 17

WARRANTY NOTES: NEXT TIME YOU NEED ENCOURAGEMENT, WAIT BEFORE THE LORD AND SEE IF HE DOESN'T HAVE A SPECIAL WORD OF ENCOURAGEMENT FOR YOU.

Dear God,
Forgive me for forgetting that the
best source of encouragement is You.
Right now I ask You to encourage
my heart as only You can.
Amen.

Ten

God's

Guarantees

about His

Forgiveness

JESUS IS YOUR PEACE

I promise you that My Son, Jesus, is the One who breaks down all barriers of hostility. The peace Jesus brings doesn't recognize one group over another, but instead unites everyone. You can be sure that as long as you believe that His blood was shed so that all people could enjoy My forgiveness, His peace will always be available to you. Call on Jesus and He'll give you peace.

FROM EPHESIANS 2:13–14

WARRANTY NOTES: THE PEACE OF JESUS OVERCOMES ALL OUR DIFFERENCES.

Dear God,
When I'm hurt or angry, it's difficult to forgive others.
Help me remember that the peace of Jesus
can mend divisions in my relationships
and makes forgiveness possible.
Amen.

God Guarantees

JESUS' BLOOD CLEANSES YOU FROM ALL SIN

You can believe that My Son, Jesus, shed His blood so you could be forgiven. Material things like silver or gold weren't precious enough to redeem sins—only a pure, unblemished sacrifice could do that. Jesus, My spotless Lamb, spilled His blood in order to purchase the forgiveness of your sins. That single sacrifice was sufficient to cover everyone's sins for all time. His blood is able to cleanse any wrongs you will ever commit.

FROM HEBREWS 9:22; 1 PETER 1:18–19

WARRANTY NOTES: JESUS PAID FOR YOUR FORGIVENESS WITH HIS BLOOD.

*Dear God, it's so comforting to know that I'm forgiven through Jesus' life, death, and resurrection.
I humbly ask You to wash away my sins today by the power of Jesus' blood.
Amen.*

I Am Faithful to Forgive Your Sins

The moment you confess your sins, I am ready and waiting to forgive you. I promise not to hold things over your head or make impossible demands before I will forgive you. I ask you only to tell Me about your mistakes and ask for forgiveness so your life can be more productive. I've given My Son, Jesus, the authority to cleanse you from every wrong, and you can depend on Him.

FROM 1 JOHN 1:9

WARRANTY NOTES: GOD LISTENS TO EVERY CONFESSION OF SIN AND FORGIVES EACH ONE THROUGH JESUS.

Dear God, I've blown it—again.
But I know that when I acknowledge my mistakes,
You are faithful to forgive me through Your Son, Jesus.
So I confess my sin right now and ask You to forgive
me. Thank You for making me clean again.
Amen.

God Guarantees

JESUS IS YOUR RIGHTEOUSNESS

I promise you righteousness—that is, blameless-ness—through My Son, Jesus. I chose to manifest My righteousness through Him. Whenever you lay your sins at His feet, you will be forgiven. You can't become righteous on your own, and if you try, you'll only focus on things that don't really matter. The path to forgiveness for your sins is always through the righteousness of Jesus.

FROM 2 CORINTHIANS 5:21;
PHILIPPIANS 3:9; ROMANS 3:22

WARRANTY NOTES: GOD NOT ONLY SECURED OUR FORGIVENESS THROUGH JESUS, BUT ALSO WENT ONE STEP FARTHER BY SECUR-ING OUR ONGOING RIGHTEOUSNESS IN HIM.

Dear God, so often I feel that being forgiven means being perfect. Yet the more I try, the less perfect I know I am. Teach me, Lord, to rely on Jesus' righteousness.
Amen.

God Guarantees

I WON'T REMEMBER YOUR SINS

When I forgive you, you can be sure that I really mean it. I'm not going to bring up the past over and over—in fact, I promise that once your sin is blotted out, I'll never think about it again. After you've been forgiven, I'm not interested in rehashing each mistake you make. Because I love you, I'd rather be merciful and remember your sins no more.

FROM ISAIAH 43:25; HEBREWS 8:12

WARRANTY NOTES: WHEN YOU TALK TO GOD ABOUT SINS HE'S ALREADY FORGIVEN, IT'S AS IF HE DOESN'T EVEN KNOW WHAT YOU'RE TALKING ABOUT.

Dear God, I'm so happy that You don't keep reminding me of things I've done wrong in the past. Once You forgive me, You forget that I sinned at all. Help me forget those past sins too, so I don't keep kicking myself for things You don't even remember.
Amen.

God Guarantees

I WILL WASH YOU
WHITE AS SNOW

If you think you've done something too bad to tell Me about, think again. I assure you that there's no mistake I cannot deal with, no crime too horrible to admit to Me. Besides, I already know everything you've ever done anyway. Just confess your sins to Me so I can forgive you. Let's talk things over—I am eager to prove to you that I can remove the deepest, most stubborn stain from your life and make you as clean as freshly fallen snow.

FROM ISAIAH 1:18

WARRANTY NOTES: NO STAIN IS SO DARK AND DEEP THAT GOD CAN'T WASH IT COMPLETELY AWAY.

Dear God,
I'm convinced that Jesus knows how to wash my sins away—completely. Thank You for the assurance that He blots out my transgressions and washes me clean again.
Amen.

God Guarantees

I WILL CLEANSE YOU FROM UNRIGHTEOUSNESS

Confess all your sins to Me—I promise I will forgive you and cleanse you from unrighteousness. My Son, Jesus, died for this purpose, and He has My authority because He is My righteousness. In other words, you can depend on Him to wash away every wrong thing you'll ever do. Whether you have big sins or small sins, only Jesus has the power to forgive. Just confess.

FROM 1 JOHN 1:9

WARRANTY NOTES: GOD WANTS US TO ADMIT OUR SINS TO HIM. THE MOMENT WE SAY, "I'M GUILTY," HE SAYS, "YOU'RE FORGIVEN."

Dear God,
I believe that if I confess my sins, instead of trying to
ignore them or pretend they never happened,
You promise to forgive me and cleanse me.
Amen.

JESUS IS YOUR ADVOCATE

I know you don't want to sin, but when you do, I've appointed Jesus to help you. He'll plead your case before Me, and I promise you that since Jesus pleases Me completely, He's the best one to represent you. You can rely on My Son to speak on your behalf. You'll be justified by faith in Jesus, who took My wrath upon Himself in order to shatter your sinful nature.

FROM 1 JOHN 2:1; ROMANS 6:2–3

WARRANTY NOTES: JESUS CHRIST IS ON PERMANENT RETAINER, WAITING TO REPRESENT YOU IN FRONT OF GOD.

Dear God,
How wonderful it is to have Jesus to plead my case
when I've sinned terribly. Thank You, God, for giving
me an Advocate whom I can trust completely.
Amen.

Eleven

❧

God's Guarantees about His Power to Deliver

God Guarantees

MY TRUTH WILL
SET YOU FREE

If you continue to study and obey My Word, then you are truly My disciple. "You will know the truth, and the truth will set you free."

FROM JOHN 8:31–32

WARRANTY NOTES: JESUS' DISCIPLES ASKED WHAT HE MEANT WHEN HE SAID THAT THEY WOULD BE "SET FREE." HE ANSWERED, "EVERYONE WHO SINS IS A SLAVE TO SIN. NOW A SLAVE HAS NO PERMANENT PLACE IN THE FAMILY, BUT A SON BELONGS TO IT FOR-EVER" (JOHN 8:34–35).

Dear God,
Right now I claim for myself
this promise of freedom from sin.
I am not a slave to sin,
but because of what You have done for me,
I am a child of God who is free indeed.
Amen.

God Guarantees

THE DEVIL WILL
FLEE FROM YOU

When the devil is tempting you, resist him and instead submit to Me and take refuge in Me. Come near to Me, and I will come near to you. When you do so, I guarantee that the devil will flee from you.

FROM JAMES 4:7–8

WARRANTY NOTES: OUT THERE ON YOUR OWN, YOU LOOK LIKE THE NEXT MEAL FOR SATAN, WHO PROWLS AROUND LIKE A HUNGRY LION. BUT WHEN YOU DRAW NEAR TO GOD, SATAN TURNS INTO A SCAREDY-CAT (SEE ALSO 1 PETER 5:8).

Dear God,
Right now I choose to receive the protection You promise. If I resist You instead of Satan, I'm doomed. Instead, I am even now drawing near to You, and I ask You to draw near to me so that Satan will flee.
Amen.

God Guarantees

I Will Provide
a Way Out

When you face a powerful temptation, you can be sure that I will have made it possible for you to escape its grasp. All you have to do is choose to take the way out that I show you. I promise that you will never experience a temptation so powerful that you can't resist it if you truly want to.

FROM 1 CORINTHIANS 10:13

WARRANTY NOTES: GIVING IN TO TEMPTATION IS THE SAME AS GIVING UP ON GOD'S HELP.

Dear God,
Thank You for the wonderful promise
that I will never face a temptation too big for me.
If I look around and look to You,
I will discover how to escape.
Amen.

God Guarantees

I WILL INSTRUCT MY ANGELS TO GUARD YOU

You can be confident that My angels encamp around those who fear Me, and I deliver my children from every kind of trouble. If You make Me your refuge and dwell with Me, no harm will befall you and no disaster will come upon your home. For I will direct my angels to guard you in all your ways.

FROM PSALM 34:7; 91:9–11

WARRANTY NOTES: GOD'S ANGELS ARE POWERFUL SPIRITUAL BEINGS WHO DO ONLY HIS BIDDING.

Dear God,
Yes, I believe in angels.
Not the kind with pretty wings that appear on greeting cards, but the kind that You created and oversee. Please send your angels to guard me, I pray.
Amen.

MY STAFF WILL COMFORT YOU

During those times when it is dark and you walk in what feels like the shadow of death, do not fear any evil, for I am with you. Because I am your shepherd, allow My rod and My staff to comfort you, reminding you that I am fully devoted to you and powerfully equipped to protect you.

FROM PSALM 23:4

WARRANTY NOTES: DAVID WROTE THE FAMOUS TWENTY-THIRD PSALM WHEN HE WAS IN GRAVE PHYSICAL DANGER FROM HIS ENEMIES—SOMETHING MOST OF US MAY NEVER FACE. BUT EVEN THEN, HE TRUSTED IN GOD'S POWER TO PROTECT HIM.

Dear God, I believe that even when I feel the shadow of death looming, I don't need to be afraid of it or of anyone. You are my shepherd, and I will take comfort in Your protection.
Amen.

MY STRONG ARMS
WILL CARRY YOU

I come down from the heavens in incredible splendor to help you. I am a safe place that you can always turn to, and My everlasting arms are always under you. I will hold your heaviness, your burdens, your whole being. My arms are solid and fully capable of lifting you, holding you, and helping you.

FROM DEUTERONOMY 33:26–27

WARRANTY NOTES: IF WE COUNT ON GOD'S UNDERGIRDING ARMS, THEY WILL BE THERE, AND WE WILL SENSE THEM WITH OUR HEARTS.

Dear God, it is incredible that Your arms are always beneath me and will never let me go. Don't let me forget this, even in my most difficult times. Remind me to let You hold me so I can experience the safety and assurance of Your everlasting strength and support.
Amen.

I WILL GRANT YOU JUSTICE

I am a just judge. I always do what is right. I look out for the poor and oppressed. I chose you to be my precious child, so when you call to me night and day for justice, I will see that you get it. You can trust Me to make sure that people do not treat you unfairly or take advantage of you.

FROM LUKE 18:7–8

WARRANTY NOTES: JESUS TOLD A PARABLE ABOUT A POOR WIDOW WHO KEPT PESTERING AN UNJUST JUDGE FOR JUSTICE—AND HE FINALLY LISTENED TO HER. JESUS' POINT WAS THAT WE SHOULD PERSEVERE IN PRAYER, KNOWING THAT, UNLIKE THE UNJUST JUDGE, GOD WILL RESPOND.

Dear God, I come before You morning after morning knowing that You will answer my prayers. Thank You for the strength to persevere.
Amen.

God Guarantees

YOU WILL OVERCOME

Because you are My child and have been born of Me, your faith will be able to overcome the world and its temptations. The source of your victory lies in your faith in Jesus Christ. Because you believe that He is My Son, you can rest assured that your faith will ultimately overcome any opposition.

FROM 1 JOHN 5:4

WARRANTY NOTES: EVEN WHEN IT LOOKS LIKE YOU ARE LOSING A BATTLE, GOD PROMISES THAT YOUR FAITH IS GREAT ENOUGH TO CONQUER ANYTHING THAT COMES YOUR WAY.

Dear God,
I trust You to bring me victory
in my situation with _____.
Because of my faith in You, I know that You will
provide the power I need to overcome.
With You on my side, I will be victorious.
Amen.

God Guarantees

I AM YOUR STRONGHOLD

When trouble threatens, the only source of salvation is in Me. If you strive to live a righteous life, I promise that you will find Me to be a stronghold—a place of power and safety—in times of trouble. I will help you and deliver you from your enemies. I will save you because you take refuge in Me.

FROM PSALM 37:39–40

WARRANTY NOTES: IMAGINE THE THICKEST, STRONGEST FORT IN THE HISTORY OF HUMAN WAR, BRISTLING WITH ARMAMENT. GOD'S REFUGE IS STRONGER. RUN TO HIM WHEN YOU NEED PROTECTION OR DELIVERANCE.

Dear God,
I believe that you are my stronghold in times of trouble.
I will take refuge in You; I will hide within Your walls,
confident that with You on my side, I am safe.
Amen.

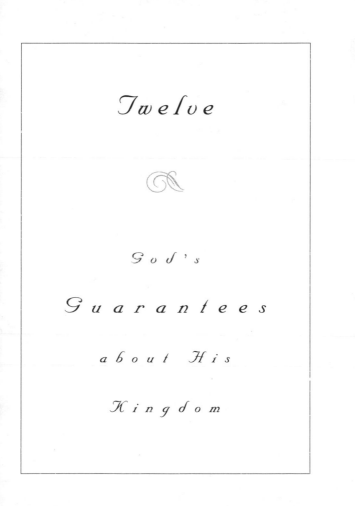

Twelve

God's

Guarantees

about His

Kingdom

God Guarantees

YOU WILL FIND
YOUR LIFE

If you cling to your life and work hard to hold on to what you have, you will end up losing everything. But if you surrender your life to Me, if you are willing to give up your life for My sake, you will ultimately find and enjoy your life.

FROM MATTHEW 10:39

WARRANTY NOTES: AS IS OFTEN THE CASE, GOD'S PRINCIPLES REQUIRE US TO DO THE OPPOSITE OF WHAT COMES NATURALLY TO OUR CARNAL NATURE.

Dear God,
Show me how to lose my life for Your sake.
Because I believe Your promise, I want to hold my life
loosely, always ready to surrender any part of it to You.
I know that only then will I truly
find life as You intended.
Amen.

I WILL RESTORE WHAT YOU SACRIFICE

I tell you the truth. If you leave home or brothers or sisters or mother or father or children or possessions or wealth for My gospel's sake, you will surely receive a hundred times as much in this present age and in the age to come, eternal life. But those who are first here on earth will find themselves in last place in heaven, and the last on earth will be first in heaven.

FROM MARK 10:29–31

WARRANTY NOTES: WHATEVER A CHRISTIAN GIVES UP FOR CHRIST WILL ALWAYS BE RESTORED TO HIM IN SOME GREATER, MORE GLORIOUS FORM.

Dear God, sometimes it is hard to make sacrifices for Your sake because I am so now-centered and so me-centered. Forgive me. Help me, by Your grace, to make generous sacrifices for You.

Amen.

God Guarantees

MY KINGDOM LIES WITHIN YOU

My kingdom is not something you can observe and point to, nor is it something about which people can say, "Here it is," or "There it is." That's because the kingdom of God is spiritual. I promise that My kingdom lies within you and within the hearts of all who love Me.

FROM LUKE 17:20–21

WARRANTY NOTES: JESUS' DISCIPLES WERE CONFUSED ABOUT GOD'S KINGDOM, ASSUMING THAT IT WOULD LOOK LIKE AN EARTHLY KINGDOM. BUT GOD WAS SETTING UP HIS HEAVENLY KINGDOM, WHERE JESUS IS THE LORD OF OUR ETERNAL SOULS.

Dear God, how amazing it is to think that You live inside me and that the reign of Your kingdom happens in my heart. May I honor You as My king and give You the glory due Your name.
Amen.

MY KINGDOM BELONGS
TO CHILDREN

When you think about the kingdom of God, remember that it belongs to those who come to Me like children—humbly, openly, ready to trust Me. You can't enter My kingdom any other way. But I promise that if you come to Me as a child would, My kingdom truly belongs to you.

FROM LUKE 18:16–17

**WARRANTY NOTES: THERE IS A BIG DIFFER-
ENCE BETWEEN BEING CHILDISH AND BEING
CHILDLIKE (SEE 1 CORINTHIANS 13:11).**

Dear God,
Thank You for inviting me to come to You with
childlike trust and faith. Right now I lay aside all my
tendencies to be cynical, conniving, or arrogant.
Please receive me as Your child
and welcome me into Your kingdom.
Amen.

YOU MUST BE BORN AGAIN

No one can enter My kingdom unless he is born again. I don't mean this in the physical sense, but in the spiritual sense. When you decide to receive Me, your eternal soul is born all over again by water and by My Spirit. You become a new creature from within and a member of My kingdom.

FROM JOHN 3:5; 2 CORINTHIANS 5:17

WARRANTY NOTES: JUST AS WE ARE BORN BY OUR MOTHER INTO A PHYSICAL FAMILY, WE ARE BORN BY GOD INTO HIS ETERNAL FAMILY.

Dear God,
I rejoice to know that the minute I received Your
forgiveness and salvation, You didn't just patch me up;
You gave me a completely fresh start,
just like a newborn babe.
Thank You for this miracle.
Amen.

God Guarantees

YOUR REWARD
WILL BE GREAT

What spiritual credit is it to you if you love those who love you? Or if you lend money to people who you are certain will pay you back? Even unbelievers do those things. I'm asking you to love those who don't love you, even your enemies. I'm asking you to give to those who can't repay you. If you do these things, your reward will be great and you will be My true sons and daughters.

FROM LUKE 6:32–35

WARRANTY NOTES: THE WAYS OF GOD OFTEN REQUIRE BEHAVIOR THAT IS THE TOTAL OPPOSITE OF WHAT COMES NATURALLY TO US.

Dear God, Your ways are so much better than mine. Still, it is hard to do the right thing—or to even see that I'm not doing it. Help me act in such a way that I live like someone who has hope of heaven. Make me a person whose every action reflects an eternal, godly perspective.
Amen.

God Guarantees

YOU CANNOT SERVE TWO MASTERS

No servant can be devoted to two masters. It's just not possible. You will either hate the one and love the other, or be devoted to one and despise the other. The same is true when it comes to money. You cannot serve both money and Me at the same time. You must choose which will be your master.

FROM LUKE 16:13

WARRANTY NOTES: IT IS EXTREMELY DIFFICULT FOR THE RICH TO ENTER HIS KINGDOM (SEE MATTHEW 19:23). THAT'S BECAUSE THE MORE MONEY WE HAVE, THE MORE WE WANT IT, FOCUS ON IT, AND PLACE OUR TRUST IN IT.

Dear Lord, I believe that You want to give me the good things that money can buy, but You don't want me to love and serve those things. Right now I choose the freedom and joy that comes from serving You alone. Please give me only what You want me to have.
Amen.

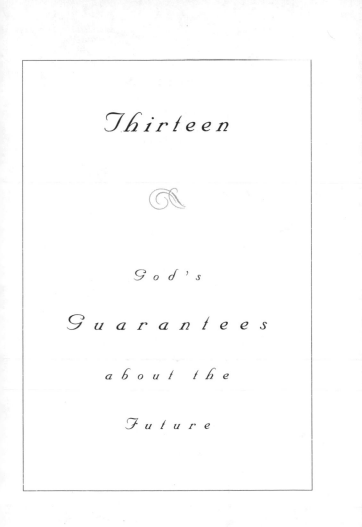

Thirteen

God's

Guarantees

about the

Future

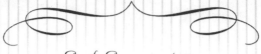

God Guarantees

I HAVE A FUTURE
FOR YOU

I want you to know that My intentions for you are good. I want to bring you peace, not turmoil. I want to give you hope and a future. In light of this, call upon Me and pray to Me, and I promise that I will listen to you. Whenever you look for Me, you'll find Me, as long as you are seeking Me with all your heart.

FROM JEREMIAH 29:11–13

WARRANTY NOTES: GOD HAS BRIGHT PLANS FOR YOUR FUTURE, BUT YOU MUST SEEK HIM TO FIND THEM.

Dear God, I believe that You have good things in mind for my future. How I long to experience the peace and hope You promise! I will seek You with all my heart, knowing that then I will not miss You and all You have planned for my life.
Amen.

God Guarantees

I AM ALWAYS WITH YOU

In the days to come, if ever you feel lonely or lost, rest assured that I am not only nearby, but I am also wholly present with you. If you love Me, I promise to be with you in a tangible way that you will feel and know. I have sent My Holy Spirit not only to comfort you and counsel you with My truths, but also to be as close to you as is possible—to live within you forever. You are not alone, My child.

FROM JOHN 14:15–18

WARRANTY NOTES: IF YOU'RE HAVING TROUBLE SENSING GOD'S PRESENCE, SLOW DOWN AND BE QUIET. GOD SAYS, "BE STILL, AND KNOW THAT I AM GOD!" (PSALM 46:10).

Dear God,
Thank You for sending Your
Holy Spirit to reside in my heart.
Right now I ask for His comforting presence,
fully believing that it is already mine.
Amen.

God Guarantees

OLD THINGS HAVE
PASSED AWAY

If you have Christ living inside you, you are a whole new creation. Your old ways of thinking and behaving have truly passed away. Become convinced that the past has no power over you now. Believe Me, your past has vanished. All things—past, present, and future—have been made new for you.

FROM 2 CORINTHIANS 5:17

WARRANTY NOTES: YOU MIGHT STILL DO SOME OF THE SAME THINGS YOU DID BEFORE YOU RECEIVED SALVATION, BUT YOU AREN'T THE SAME PERSON. YOU ARE A NEW CREATION IN CHRIST WHO HAS AN ENTIRELY NEW FUTURE AHEAD.

Dear God, I am so glad that when You saved me from my sins and gave me eternal life, You also promised to give me a completely new start and a bright, promising future. I praise You for this and rejoice in my newness of life.

Amen.

God Guarantees

I WILL BRING YOU
HOME TO BE WITH ME

Do not let your heart be troubled, but trust in Me. In My house there are many rooms and plenty of space for all My children. I am even now preparing a place just for you. I promise that one day I will come for you and bring you home with Me. We will be together always.

FROM JOHN 14:1–3

WARRANTY NOTES: JESUS' DISCIPLES WERE DEEPLY CONCERNED WHEN HE TALKED ABOUT LEAVING THEM. TO COMFORT THEM, HE EXPLAINED THAT SOMEDAY HE WOULD SURELY COME BACK FOR THEM—AND FOR US.

Dear God, how good it is to remember that
You are coming back for me. I believe Your promise
that it won't always be like this, with You in
heaven and me waiting for You here on earth.
I can hardly wait to go home with You.
Amen.

I Am Not Slow in Keeping My Promise

Here is something to keep in mind: With Me, a day is like a thousand years and a thousand years is like a day. I am not slow when it comes to keeping My promise to return for you, as some people might understand slowness. Rather, I am patient with the world, because I don't want any person to perish, but all to come to repentance and be saved.

FROM 2 PETER 3:8–9

WARRANTY NOTES: GOD DOES NOT VIEW TIME AS WE DO BECAUSE GOD IS NOT SUBJECT TO TIME THE WAY WE ARE. FOR HIM, THE FUTURE IS AS GOOD AS HERE.

Dear God, what we take for slowness is a loving delay on Your part, because You want to save as many people as possible. I believe what You say, and I thank You for it. Help me lead others to know You, and give me greater patience, I pray.

Amen.

God Guarantees

YOU SHALL NEVER DIE

I am the resurrection and the life. If you believe in Me, even though your physical body dies, you will nevertheless live. Whoever lives and believes in Me will never die.

FROM JOHN 11:25–26

WARRANTY NOTES: JESUS SPOKE THESE WORDS TO MARTHA JUST BEFORE HE RAISED LAZARUS FROM THE GRAVE, PROVING THAT HE TRULY DOES HAVE POWER OVER DEATH. THOUGH YOUR FUTURE INCLUDES THE PHYSICAL DEATH OF YOUR BODY, IT DOESN'T INCLUDE YOUR SPIRITUAL DEATH— THE DEATH OF WHO YOU ARE.

Dear God,
Because You overcame death,
I no longer have to fear it.
I believe that my life will continue forever,
and I thank You for this amazing promise.
Amen.

God Guarantees

YOU HAVE AN
INHERITANCE IN HEAVEN

Because of My great mercy, I have given You a living hope through the resurrection of My Son, Jesus Christ. I assure you that through Him you have a priceless inheritance that is incorruptible, unspoiled, and unfading. And this inheritance is reserved especially for you in heaven.

FROM 1 PETER 1:3–4

WARRANTY NOTES: AN EARTHLY INHERITANCE FROM OUR PARENTS PALES WHEN COMPARED TO WHAT OUR HEAVENLY FATHER PLANS TO PASS ON TO US IN THE FUTURE (SEE EPHESIANS 1:11–14).

Dear God, thank You for the assurance that
I have a glorious inheritance waiting for me in heaven,
one that no stock market dip could dent,
that no contested will could deny me.
I rejoice in knowing that I am forever Your heir.
Amen.

God Guarantees

I WILL FINISH WHAT
I BEGAN IN YOU

The spiritual work I began within you the moment you received Me is not finished yet. Be confident in Me, the One who initiated this work, and trust in Me to bring to completion all the growth and progress that I have begun in your heart and life.

FROM PHILIPPIANS 1:6

WARRANTY NOTES: GOD IS NEVER FINISHED MOLDING AND SHAPING US UNTIL HE CALLS US HOME.

Dear God,
I'm so glad that You never give up on me and say,
"Forget this. There's just no hope for this one."
I believe that You will indeed continue to be at
work in my life, helping me to become all that
You had in mind for me when You created me.
Amen.

God Guarantees

I WILL USE EVERYTHING FOR YOUR GOOD

If you walk in My ways and share My purposes, then no matter what happens in your life, I promise that I will use it to bring about something positive. I always cause all things to ultimately work together for good for those who love Me.

FROM ROMANS 8:28

WARRANTY NOTES: WHEN JACOB'S SON JOSEPH RECONCILED WITH HIS OLDER BROTHERS, WHO HAD HORRIBLY BETRAYED HIM, HE POINTED OUT THAT WHAT THEY HAD INTENDED FOR EVIL, GOD HAD INTENDED FOR GOOD (SEE GENESIS 50:20).

Dear God, I believe that no matter what happens in my future, I can rest assured that if I cooperate with Your purposes, You will be at work to make everything I experience result in something good.
Thank You, Lord.
Amen.